Weird, wild, and wonderful

Frogs

D1606715

Gareth Stevens
Publishing

By Gary Underwood

Please visit our Web site **www.garethstevens.com.** For a free color catalog of all our high-quality books, call toll free 1-800-542-2595 or fax 1-877-542-2596.

Library of Congress Cataloging-in-Publication Data

Underwood, Gary.
 Frogs / Gary Underwood.
    p. cm. — (Weird, wild, and wonderful)
 Includes index.
 ISBN 978-1-4339-3578-7 (library binding)
 1. Frogs—Juvenile literature. I. Title.
 QL668.E2U53 2010
 597.8′9—dc22
                                    2009043971

Published in 2010 by
Gareth Stevens Publishing
111 East 14th Street, Suite 349
New York, NY 10003

For Gareth Stevens Publishing:
Art Direction: Haley Harasymiw
Editorial Direction: Kerri O'Donnell

Designed in Australia by www.design-ed.com.au

Photography by Kathie Atkinson
Additional photographs: Photolibrary, p. 15; © iStockphotos.com/Kitch Bain, p. 17; © iStockphotos.com/Nick Watts, p. 18; © iStockphotos.com/phil morley, p. 22.

Printed in the United States of America

CPSIA compliance information: Batch #CW10GS: For further information contact Gareth Stevens, New York, New York, at 1-800-542-2595.

Contents

What Are Frogs?

A frog is an amphibian. This means it spends part of its life in water and part on land. A frog is a **vertebrate**. It has a backbone. It is **cold-blooded** with smooth, slimy skin. Frogs live where there is water. Frogs are **carnivores**. They eat other animals.

These green reed frogs use their feet and fingers to climb wet, slippery reeds.

Frogs are cold-blooded. That means their body is about as hot or cold as the air around it.

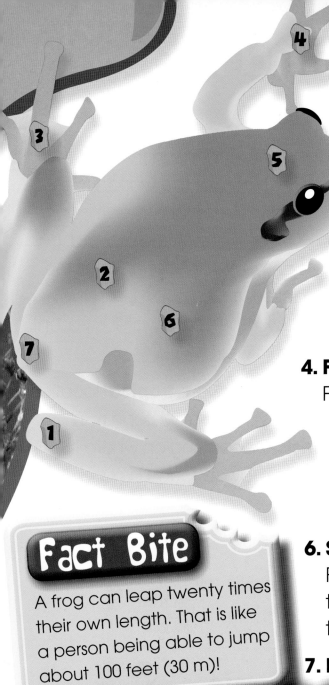

The body of a frog has a number of special features.

1. Long, strong back legs
These long legs means the frog can jump on land and swim in water.

2. A short body

3. Webbed feet
Webs help them move through the water.

4. Fingers
Frogs have pads on the tips of their fingers. This helps them grip surfaces.

5. Bulging eyes
These eyes help the frog see in any direction.

6. Smooth, slimy skin
Frogs can **absorb** water and oxygen through their skin. They also have lungs to breathe.

7. No tail!

Fact Bite

A frog can leap twenty times their own length. That is like a person being able to jump about 100 feet (30 m)!

Where Do You Find Frogs?

This large, tropical green tree frog has found a flowerpot to hide in.

Frogs can be found in the wild around most of the world. Frogs need to live near water. It can be a lot of water, like in a pond. It can be a little water, like in the desert. It can even be in the snow where the water is frozen! That's weird!

Most frogs live in **tropical** locations. There is plenty of water in **rain forests**. Depending on where they live, frogs may be found around waterways, up trees, or under the ground.

Fact Bite

These marks are left on the ground by a frog. They are belly and toe marks.

You can also find frogs near garden ponds, small streams, and **marshes**. Where there is water, there may be frogs.

Frogs do not need to drink water. They have a wonderful way of soaking up water through their skin.

Desert frogs survive with very little water.

In the snow, the water is frozen. These frogs **hibernate** through the winter.

7

Croaky Romance

Adult frogs gather at ponds or streams to **breed**. Some go back to where they were born. The male frog calls out to attract a **mate**. Each species, or kind, has its own special call.

Some frog croaks are loud. They can be heard a half mile (1 k) away.

This male striped marsh frog is calling for a mate. He swells up his throat to make his croak louder.

A garden pond is a good spot for males to meet females.

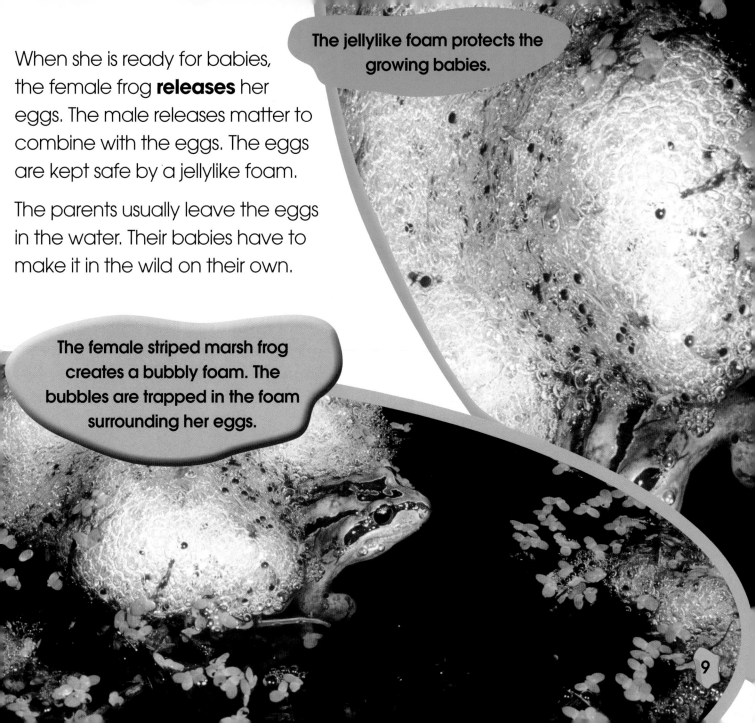

When she is ready for babies, the female frog **releases** her eggs. The male releases matter to combine with the eggs. The eggs are kept safe by a jellylike foam.

The parents usually leave the eggs in the water. Their babies have to make it in the wild on their own.

The jellylike foam protects the growing babies.

The female striped marsh frog creates a bubbly foam. The bubbles are trapped in the foam surrounding her eggs.

Are Tadpoles Fish?

Tadpoles form inside the eggs. They will stay in the eggs for several weeks. Then they will **hatch**.

Tadpoles are forming inside the eggs.

Fact Bite

Frog eggs make good food for wild birds, fish, and bugs. If the water dries up, the eggs dry out and die. If the water is polluted, the eggs will die. So frogs lay lots of eggs.

Fish eggs

The baby tadpoles have very long tails. Most tadpoles start to swim as soon as they hatch.

Tadpoles are like weird little fish. They have **gills**. They can only breathe underwater.

Some tadpoles are **herbivores**. They only eat plants and **algae**. Others eat meat as well.

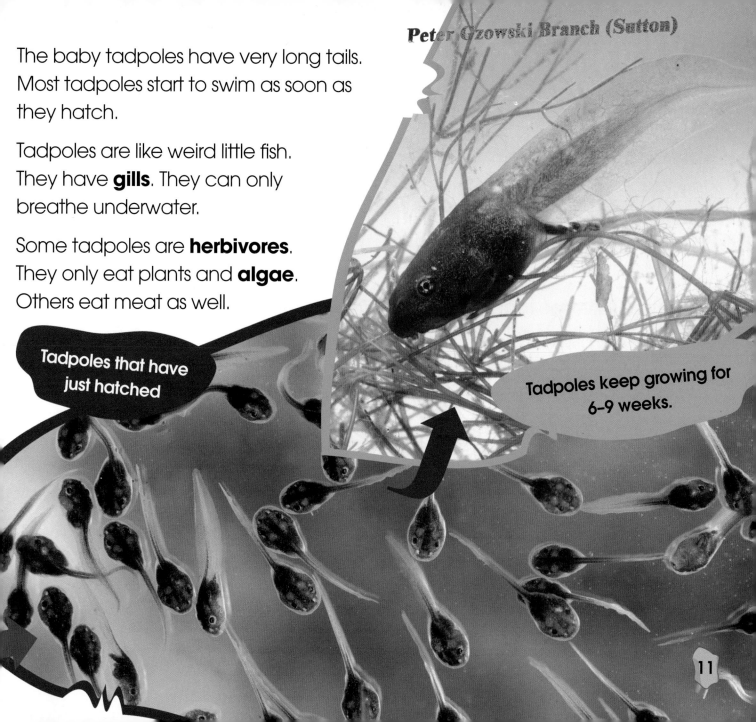

Tadpoles that have just hatched

Tadpoles keep growing for 6–9 weeks.

11

Who Stole My Tail?

After a few months, the tiny tadpole starts to change. Its body gets longer. It loses its gills. It grows lungs. Then it grows legs. Weird!

Sometime later, the tadpole starts to look like a small frog. It still has a long tail. Its eyes change position.

The young frog still has a bit of its tail. It starts to crawl out of the water. Now, it eats only meat.

At 6 weeks

At 9 weeks

After a number of months, the frog is fully grown. Its tail is completely gone! It leaves the water. It will only come back to breed or to soak in the water.

At 16 weeks

At 13 weeks

Fact Bites

When a frog swallows its food, its huge eyeballs are pushed down into its head. This pushes the food down its throat. Wild!

13

A Flick of the Tongue

Frogs like to eat wild insects that are moving. A frog has a very long tongue. It can "zap" out, catch a bug, and then "zap" back in. This happens in less than a second. It is so fast, the bug doesn't even see it coming.

The frog's long tongue will be able to reach the spider easily.

Fact Bite

A frog's tongue can move too fast to see.

A frog's tongue can be 4 inches (10 cm) long. It has a sticky end to help grab its meal. The frog's tongue is joined to the front of the jaw, not the back of the throat. That is the opposite of most animals' tongues. The frog's tongue has a very strong muscle down the middle.

This grasshopper was caught by the frog's fast tongue.

The frog's tongue shoots like a rocket out of its mouth.

Where Am I?

Many frogs use **camouflage** to stay safe. Frogs can be different colors. The colors and patterns match their surroundings. This helps them blend in.

Some frogs are shaped like leaves. They are very hard to see. That helps them hide from their enemies. This is very important during the day, when they sleep. It also helps them hide when they look for food.

Frogs sleep during the day.

16

This frog has smooth skin. It looks like a leaf on this tree branch.

Some frogs have weird warts (bumps) and folds on their skin that help them hide on branches. Others have smooth skin like the leaves they hide in. Some frogs change color between night and day.

The warts on this frog make it look like a branch.

Frogs in Trees

Some wild frogs live in trees! There are many types of tree frogs. They can be very different in shape and size.

Some tree frogs can climb smooth surfaces. They use their belly skin and special pads on their toes. The pads stick to the tree!

This frog has very long legs and narrow toes. They are great for climbing.

Some tree frogs walk as well as hop.

Some frogs live high up in trees. They have webbed feet. Their feet allow them to "glide" from one part of the tree to another. The webs slow them down so they don't fall to the ground.

Fact Bite

The green tree frog is popular as a pet. One lived to 23 years old!

The Roth's tree frog has long legs that help it climb.

Toe pads hold the red-eyed tree frog onto surfaces.

Can Frogs Live in Deserts?

Some frogs live in the desert. Life is hard because it is very hot and dry there. Desert frogs have different ways to cope.

The water-holding frog spends most of its life underground. It stores water under its skin. It also stores water in its **bladder**. It seals itself in a cocoon. The cocoon is made from skin cells that form thin sheets around the frog.

The water-holding frog soaks up water from the mud.

Fact Bite

Frogs don't drink. They take water in through holes in their skin.

The desert burrowing frog uses its back legs to dig down into damp sand.

The desert burrowing frog looks very round. This is because of the water stored under its skin.

Desert frogs also hide from the desert heat. They bury themselves in dry river beds. **Burrowing** frogs dig down backwards into the sand. They dig until they find a **moist** spot. They sleep there. When it rains, they wake up. They climb out to feed and breed. Wild!

21

Frog Songs

In some kinds of frog, only males can croak or make a noise. In others, both males and females can call out. The bigger the frog, the deeper the voice. The smaller the frog, the higher the voice.

In cold areas, frogs call more slowly than in warmer areas. Their muscles slow down in the cold.

Frogs call out for lots of reasons:

- to attract a mate
- to mark their territory
- to scare away enemies or when they are hurt.

They even call to tell others they think it might rain!

Fact Bite

Each kind of frog has its own call. There are hundreds of Web sites where you can listen to frogs. Try to find out what the frogs in your area sound like.

This green tree frog is puffed up to croak.

Glossary

absorb to take in something, like water, and hold it inside

algae plantlike things that grow in water

bladder the body part that holds wastewater until it is released

breed to make babies

burrowing having to do with digging holes in the ground

camouflage making the body look like the surroundings

carnivores animals that feed on other animals

cold-blooded an animal whose body is about as hot or cold as the air around it

gills organs used for breathing in water

hatch to come out of an egg

herbivores animals that eat only plants

hibernate to spend the winter in a sleeplike state

marsh wet land where grasses grow

mate (a) a breeding partner

moist a little wet

rain forests forests in the hot part of the world that receive plenty of rain

release to let go

tropical hot part of the world

vertebrate an animal that has a backbone

webs thin skin between an animal's toes

For Further Information

Books

Moffett, Mark. *Face to Face with Frogs*. Des Moines, IA: National Geographic Children's Books, 2008.

Turner, Pamela S. *The Frog Scientist*. New York: Houghton Mifflin Books for Children, 2009.

Web Sites

Exploratorium: Frogs
http://www.exploratorium.edu/frogs/

KidZone: Frogs
http://www.kidzone.ws/lw/frogs/

Publisher's note to educators and parents: Our editors have carefully reviewed these Web sites to ensure that they are suitable for students. Many Web sites change frequently, however, and we cannot guarantee that a site's future contents will continue to meet our high standards of quality and educational value. Be advised that students should be closely supervised whenever they access the Internet.

Index